The Johnson Wit

The
Johnson
Wit

Edited by

FRANCES SPATZ LEIGHTON

THE CITADEL PRESS

NEW YORK

Editor's Note

Nobody can "shoot from the lip" or tell Texas-type stories like the tall Texan in the White House. If the audience is laughing hard enough, the President can enlarge upon a story for fully fifteen minutes; he can, on the other hand, shoot an opponent down in an instant with a single sharp humorous retort.

For the reader's convenience, the material in this book has been arranged in alphabetical order according to categories. LBJ stories, for fullest effect, should be read aloud, and that is what I recommend.

FRANCES SPATZ LEIGHTON
Washington, D. C.

Contents

The Johnson Wit

Advice

I see in the papers that Barry and Rocky have decided to cut down on their appearances in California.

This reminds me of the fellow down in Texas who said to his friend, "Earl, I am thinking of running for Sheriff against Uncle Jim Wilson. What do you think?"

"Well," said his friend, "It depends on which one of you sees the most people."

"That is what I figure," said his friend.

"If you see the most, Uncle Jim will win. If he sees the most, you will win."

Fund-Raising Dinner
of the Democratic
Club of Cook County
Chicago, April 23, 1964

As Calvin Coolidge said, "You don't have to explain what you don't say."

Favorite Johson quip
of Maurice Silverman,
Justice Department

11

Whenever he is trying to epitomize the "brass collar" politician, the down-the-line organization man, Johnson tells this story:

A Senator who was a bachelor and also a part of the state political machine—a man who spent his whole lifetime going down the line with the boys,—got caught in a Washington apartment house with a woman, and he was coming up for re-election shortly.

It looked like the scandal had him knocked off. So his advisors got together and said to him, "Well Senator, there's only one answer to this. You've got to get married. That will quiet the women back home in the district and maybe they'll forget about the scandal."

So the old Senator heaved a deep sigh and said, "Well boys, it's a terrible sacrifice but I realize you are right. I'll go ahead and get married. Whom does the organization recommend?"

A favorite LBJ story of Congressman William Ayres of Ohio

Appointments

Telling about how he'd appointed Governor Buford Ellington to be Director of the Office of Emergency Planning, the President said:

I was so proud to have the Governor aboard I spent several days congratulating myself to all who would listen, and finally several nights ago I told Buford I wanted to make a speech about him when he had a swearing-in ceremony in a week or so—and Buford looked a little ill. He went ahead and finished his supper and after he completed his dessert he looked up at me and said, "Mr. President, I have already been sworn in and I'm on the job."

Cabinet Room, The White House
March 4, 1965

The President set a new style in making re-appointments. When District Commissioner Walter Tobriner sent in the customary letter of resignation at the end of his term of office, the President told him:

I couldn't read the writing in your letter—and therefore I tore it up.

March, 1965

Just last week, both Nelson Rockefeller and Barry Goldwater came to see me about a job. I had to turn both of them down because neither of them had gotten enough votes to be an ambassador.

After New Hampshire
Presidential primary, 1964

Appreciation and Gratitude

I am like the man who appreciates what you have done that Senator Barkley used to talk about all the time.

You will remember, he went home and a fellow came up to him. The Senator asked him to vote for him, and he wasn't quite sure he could do it. He was still considering it.

The Senator said, "John, I can't understand it. I appointed your brother postmaster, I appointed your sister in my office, I sent your son to West Point, and all through the years we have been friends. Now here, in the twilight of my career, when I need you most, you tell me you are not sure. What could have happened?"

The man said, "Well, Senator, you haven't done anything for me lately."

Before Treasury Agency heads
Rose Garden, The White House
April 21, 1964

This is a moment that I deeply wish my parents could have lived to share. In the first place, my father would have enjoyed what you so generously said of me and my mother would have believed it.

Address at Baylor University, Waco, Texas,
upon receipt of honorary Doctor of Laws degree
May 28, 1965

Beagles, Bagels and Photographers

LBJ got beagle-deep in trouble when a group of financial experts were visiting the White House in April, 1964. He took the men for the traditional walk around the White House lawn, ran into his beagles and lifted them by the ears to show how they yelp.

"You see what a dog will do when he gets into a crowd of bankers?" asked the President, laughing.

The Washington Post,
April 28, 1964

Some of you may know that I almost did not make it here today. Mr. Potofsky* called me and said, "Mr. President, I am afraid I will have to ask you not to come to New York Saturday."

I asked him why, and he said, "Well, Mr. President, these people are pretty mad because you pulled the ears of a 'bagel.'" But here I am among fine friends and good neighbors and out of the dog house finally, at least for the time being.

I read that man is the only animal that has a legislature. Well, I found out one thing—beagles have a constituency.

* Jacob Potofsky, President of the Amalgamated Clothing Workers of America.

And unless you have one, you really don't know how to handle them—but you are long on advice.

Singer Bowl
New York World's Fair
May 9, 1964

Some time after the ear-pulling incident, he was strolling near the White House fence while tourists watched. The President spotted his beagles and bent down to pet them. Stroking their ears, he said loudly enough for everyone to hear:

Don't yelp now or they'll quote you.

If the photographers will leave my dog alone, I will go on and finish this speech. They will be blaming me for that before it is over and saying I am talking too loud or too low, but I think that is a UP photographer. The AP photographer is better trained. I mean they have specialized in dogs over a longer period of time.

Remarks before a group
of Peace Corps volunteers,
Flower Garden, The White House,
May 16, 1964

The President had endured the cameramen and the television photographers for some time during one session, when he finally was ready to stop, but again they asked for "just one more." He endured a little more, and finally said wryly:

I never see these pictures. You must be keeping them for home movies.

A favorite LBJ anecdote of Francis Miller, Life Magazine photographer

Big Business

Finally I would say to you this: Whatever else you have—and you may not have much this morning—but you can go home and tell your friends that you have an independent, taxpaying, light-bill-saving President in the White House.

I must get back to my work at the White House and, I guess, let you get back to your work on me.

U.S. Chamber of Commerce
April 27, 1964

Campaign Humor

During the campaign of 1964, President Johnson visited the World's Fair in New York and rode with Senator Kenneth B. Keating, who was running for re-election in the state.

Johnson said, "I am worried about your health, Ken."

"But my health's fine, Mr. President," the Senator said, startled. "What gave you the notion I've been sick?"

"I just assumed it," answered the President, "when I heard that there was a Bar Mitzvah in Schenectady, with fourteen people, and you didn't show up."

New York Post,
May 25, 1964

We meet in a historic hall tonight. In this very spot will be chosen an American leader for 1965, a person who symbolizes the American dream. I am sad that it becomes my duty to announce tonight that that person will not be me. [*dramatic pause*] It will be Miss America of 1965.

Convention Hall
Atlantic City
May 9, 1964

I don't want to be partisan. I don't want to be political. I am President. I haven't had much political experience, but I am President of all the people, Democrats and Republicans. Therefore, I just want to say that I hope that whatever candidate of whatever party is chosen in this hall will be successful next November.

Convention Hall
Atlantic City
May 9, 1964

A lot of Republicans have not decided who they want to be their nominee.

One old man was asked how he was going to vote in the California primary. He said, "Well, I haven't decided yet, but I will tell you this: When I do make up my mind, I am going to be awfully bitter."

And I think that is the dilemma that the Republicans face.

Fund-raising Dinner
Democratic Club of Cook County
Chicago
April 23, 1964

It is naturally to be assumed that I would recommend myself most highly.

Well, I will tell you a little story before I go home. This happened down in my country. We lived out on a cotton farm when I was a boy, and we had a ranch hand there who left a little after lunch one day and went over to the Old Settlers' Reunion, the Old Confederate Reunion, and he didn't come back until dark that night, just about weighing-in time, just about the time we were unloading our sacks and weighing in.

And the boss said, "Where in the world have you been all afternoon?"

He said, "I have been over to the Old Confederate Reunion."

The boss said, "What did you do all afternoon at the Confederate Reunion?"

The boy said, "Well, I listened to a United States Senator make a speech."

The boss said, "Well, the Senator didn't speak all evening, did he?"

The boy said, "Mighty near, mighty near."

The boss said, "Who was the Senator and what did he speak that long about?"

"Well," the boy said, "Boss, his name was Senator Joseph Welden Bailey, from Texas, and I don't recall precisely all the Senator talked about, but the general impression I got all afternoon was that he was recommending himself most highly."

Steps of State Capitol
Columbia, South Carolina
October 26, 1964

This is the final comment of Senator Goldwater. I don't want to criticize him and I am not going to say an unkind word about a single personality. As a matter of fact, I want to read what Senator Goldwater said and then conclude. He said, "I wouldn't comment in detail until I have read it." Normally you would want to read something before you talked about it. But he said, "It is my impression that he out-Roosevelt'd Roosevelt, and he out-Kennedy'd Kennedy and even made Truman look like a piker." What finer compliment could be paid?

Democratic National Committee Reception
The White House
January 11, 1964

I asked a fellow what had been on one of those signs and he said, "Well, we thought it was an ugly sign until

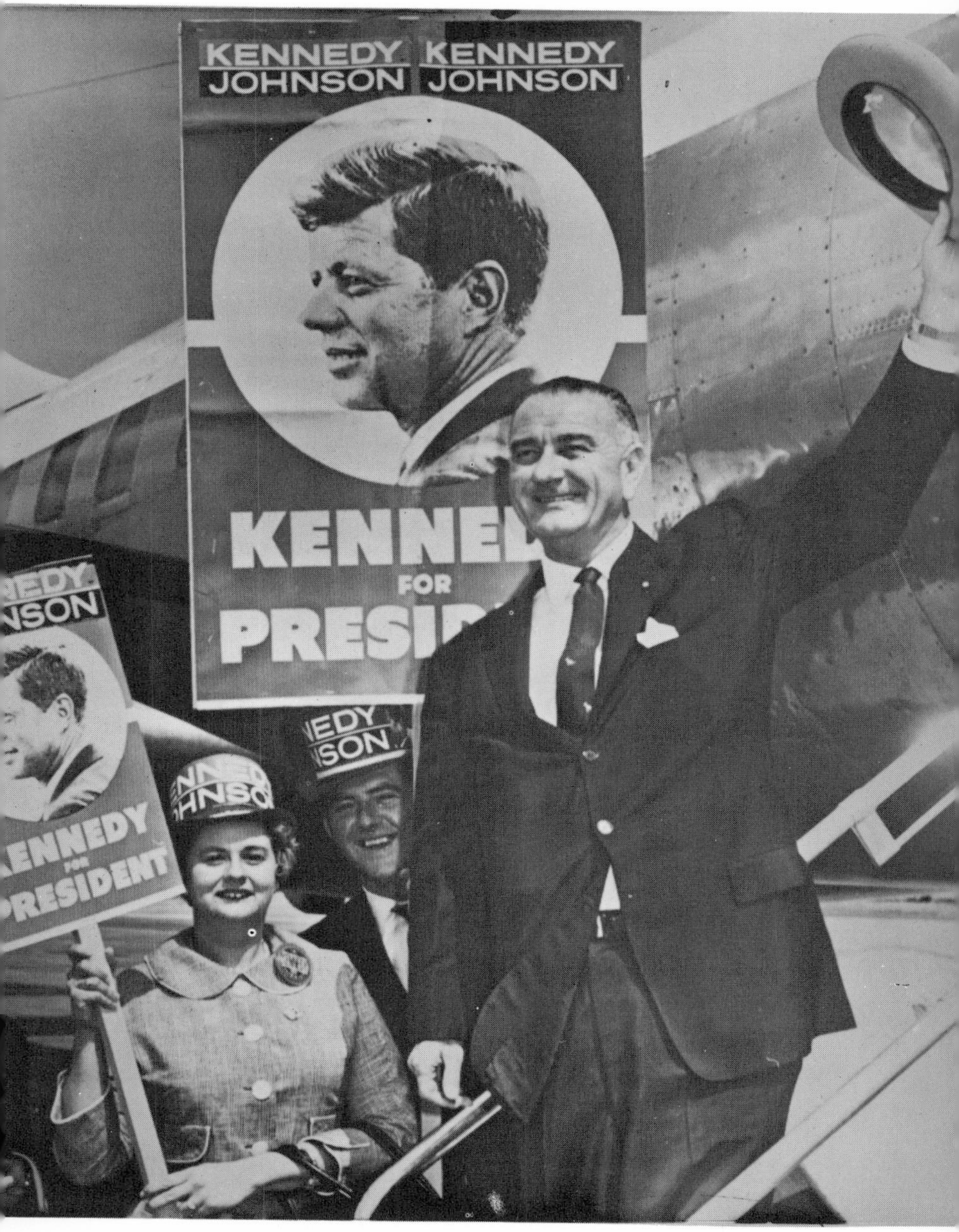
KENNEDY
JOHNSON
KENNEDY
JOHNSON
FOR
KENNEDY
FOR
RESIDENT

we got up close to where we could read. It was a home-made sign, and it said, 'Gold for the rich, and water for the poor, and Johnson for President.' "

Los Angeles
October, 1964

I hope if you do what you think is right, that some-how or other it is the same thing that I think is right. But if it is not, I won't question your patriotism. I won't question your Americanism. I won't question your ancestry.

I may, however, quietly, and in the sanctity of our bedroom, *whisper* to Lady Bird my personal opinion about your judgment.

New Orleans
October, 1964

In that previous campaign of 1960, when he was John F. Kennedy's running mate, he said many "vote-worthy" things, too, such as:

I am not going to get into the futile argument of whether Mr. Nixon did or did not participate in the decisions of the Administration. If President Eisen-hower can't recall whether he did or not, neither can I.

Tampa, Florida
October 12, 1960

We proved in the West Virginia primary that Protestants will vote for a Catholic. Now we want some of the Catholics to prove they'll vote for a Protestant.

Los Angeles
July 13, 1960

. . . American independence was not won by a philosophy of "all's well with the world and it cannot be better."

I cannot imagine George Washington standing before the Continental Congress and saying: "Gentlemen, our prestige has never been higher. The English prestige has never been lower. Let's go to Mount Vernon and play cricket."

Chicago
November 1, 1960

One of the outstanding features of this campaign has been the persistent effort of the Republican candidate to hide the Republican record. If the Republicans could help it, their record would be the best-kept secret since the atomic bomb.

During the course of the debates, the Republican Presidential candidate has spent as much time running from the Republican record as he has spent running for office.

I sympathize. . . . You might give them your sympathy too, so long as you don't make the mistake of giving them your vote.

Springfield, Mississippi
October 31, 1960

As you all may have heard, the Republican candidate for President has tried to amend the Constitution of the United States, all by himself. According to his new version, there is freedom of speech for everyone—except Democrats. He says that when Khrushchev and Castro are in this country, Jack Kennedy and I ought to keep quiet about the record of the Republican Party and its candidates.

I don't blame the Republican candidate for wanting to keep the issues out of sight until the election is over. If we had that kind of record, I would want to keep quiet about it too.

Democratic Rally
Jackson, Tennessee
September 30, 1960

One of the most interesting indoor sports in the United States is speculating on what the Republicans will promise every four years.

Do you remember a man from Vermont whose slogan was "Keep Cool with Coolidge"? It was only a matter of time until the stock market started to go up, up, up, like a fever chart.

Do you remember a man named Herbert Hoover who promised "a chicken in every pot" and "two cars in every garage?" It was only a matter of time until we couldn't even find the pot if we could scrounge the chicken.

Once again we have a Republican candidate. He promises to educate our children. He promises to develop our natural resources. He promises to solve the housing crisis. He promises to solve our farm problem. He promises to stare down the Communists in the kitchen.

It's about time we asked for these promises in writing . . . and make sure it is not written in disappearing ink.

Chattanooga, Tennessee
September 30, 1960

If I am drafted at the Democratic National Convention, I will not be a draft-dodger.

1959

Clothes Make the Man

I trust all of you will forgive me for appearing here tonight out of uniform.

The State Department and the White House have

negotiated a treaty on styles in dress—Presidents don't have to wear white ties and Ambassadors don't have to wear Texas hats.

Remarks at Reception,
for Washington Diplomatic Corps
February 11, 1965

Democracy and Government

Sometimes diplomatic negotiations recall Mark Twain's story of his visit to a friend up in New Hampshire. Mark Twain was walking along the road and he asked a farmer, "How far it is to Henderson's place?"

"About a mile and a half," the farmer answered.

He walked a while longer and met another farmer, and he again asked, "How far is it to Henderson's place?"

The farmer answered, "About a mile and a half."

Mark Twain walked a little further, met another farmer, and asked, "How far is it to Henderson's place?"

And the farmer answered, "About a mile and a half."

"Well," said Twain, "thank God, I am holding my own."

The White House
December 7, 1964

The office of Attorney General is an old office in our American system. It was one of the first four that were created, but it is a much more honored and a much more important office today then when it was first established.

The first Attorney General, Edmund Randolph, made the complaint that he was, and I quote, "a mongrel between the State and the United States." He had the title and the honor of being Attorney General of the United States, but he was left to support himself in the courts of his home state.

President Monroe some years later reminded Congress that the Attorney General had no office space and no clerk and no messenger, and he had to pay his own fuel bill and buy his own stationery.

I hesitate to observe to the Budget Director, but this might present some fine opportunities for economies that we should probably explore.

Swearing-in Ceremony
of Nicholas deB. Katzenbach
The White House
February 13, 1965

An Internal Revenue Service man telephoned a Baptist minister one day and said: "I am reviewing the tax return of one of the members of your church and he listed a donation of $200 to the church. Can you tell me if he made the contribution?" The minister replied, "I

don't have my records in front of me, but if he didn't,
he will!''

A favorite Presidential story of
Merriman Smith, United Press International

Showing how democracy works in the light bulb sit-
uation, the President told a group of public-power-
minded Texans:

The electric cooperatives were against my policy of

turning out the White House lights—until they found
out that we were serviced by *private* power.

Annual Dinner
of the Electric Cooperatives of Texas
Washington Hotel, Washington, D.C.
May 4, 1965

Education

I was a college editor once, but, as you can see, I did
not do as well as you have done, so I did the next best
thing and went into politics.

Remarks at the presentation of the
William Randolph Hearst Foundation's
Journalism Awards
May 11, 1964

My experience is like the story of the young man
whose father was asked how he made out on the
exams.

"Well," his father said, "he is doing much better. He
was almost on top of the list of those who failed."

Rose Garden, The White House
May 11, 1964

When I finished high school back in 1924, I came out

to California looking for a job. I am happy to say to you now that I am employed full-time right now. I have the best employers in the world, and when my contract is up for renewal I hope you will be satisfied with my performance.

South Gate, California
October 11, 1964

A great American, Robert Frost, once said that you never know what a young man's chances in life are going to be until you know the kind of thing for which he will neglect his studies.

Remarks to foreign student group
The White House
May 5, 1964

There is the story of a college debater who told his roommate that an upcoming debate would be a real battle of wits.

"How courageous of you," his friend said, "to go unarmed."

Accepting honorary membership
in the National Forensic League
Rose Garden, The White House
May 12, 1964

Farmers

There will be a deliberate effort to pull the wool over the eyes of the American people as the campaign continues. And this will be about the most attention the Republicans have paid to any agricultural commodity in eight years.

National Plowing Contest
Sioux Falls, South Dakota
September 20, 1960

I was once told that the difference between a farmer and an agriculturalist was that the farmer earned his money on the farm and spent it in the city, while the agriculturalist earned his money in the city and spent it on the farm.

State dinner in honor
of His Excellency, Antonio Segni,
President, Italian Republic
January 14, 1964

Feuding and Fussing

Some of you may be old enough to remember the classic story that President Roosevelt used to tell back in 1938.

It involved two feuding Irish societies whose prinicipal goal in life was to hold parades and to break up each other's parades.

The prime instrument of the parade in those days was a big bass drum.

By sheer good fortune, one of the societies acquired a beautiful new drum, bigger and better than anything that they had ever seen, even in old Ireland.

It came time for the poverty-stricken group to hold its parade.

Now Irishmen are generous, and they expect generosity from each other, so the leader of the poor society went to his wealthier brethren and asked for the loan of the great big drum.

He was told that he could have it on one condition: "Now listen, Mike, you are welcome to the drum, but it cost us a lot of money, and we could never replace it. So we are lending it to you on your personal honor that you take it out of the parade before you reach the corner of O'Connell Street, because that is where we will be laying for you."

Remarks to Friendly Sons of St. Patrick
Waldorf-Astoria Hotel, New York City
March 17, 1964

Johnson always recalls Al Smith when the subject of heckling comes up:

Once Al Smith was making a speech—or trying to— when a heckler yelled, "Tell them all you know, Al. It won't take long."

Smith pointed at the man and shouted, "Stand up,

and I'll tell them all we both know, and it won't take any longer."

Peter Lisagor
Chicago Daily News
May 9, 1964

My friend and associate Dave Powers told me on the way up here about one of the five O'Sullivan brothers.

He had just had a terrible quarrel at home and he walked to the corner and met a friend, and he said to him, "I am so angry I am going to go out and disgrace the entire family. I am going to register Republican."

Post Office Square
Boston, Massachusetts
October 27, 1964

Friendship

The names candidates call each other during the heat of a campaign brings to mind this story:

It reminds me of that judge down in Texas during the Depression, when they called him up one night and said, "Judge, we just abolished your court."

He said, "Why did you abolish my court?"

They said, "Well, we have to consolidate the courts for economy reasons. Yours was the last one created."

He said, "You didn't do it without a hearing, did you?"

They said, "Yes, we had a hearing."

He said, "Who in the devil would testify that my court ought to be abolished?"

They said, "The head of the Bar Association."

He said, "Let me tell you about the head of the Bar Association. He is a shyster lawyer and his daddy ahead of him was."

They said, "The Mayor of the city came down and testified."

The Judge said, "Let me tell you about that Mayor. He stole his way into office. He padded the ballot boxes. He counted them twice. Who else testified?"

They said, "The banker."

He said, "He has been charging usury rates like his daddy and his grand-daddy ahead of him."

They said, "Judge, we don't think we should talk any more tonight. Your blood pressure is getting up. The legislature did adjourn. Somebody did offer an amendment to abolish your court. We were kidding. No one testified against you at all. But we fought the amendment and killed it, and the bill has gone to the Governor and he signed it. We thought we would make you feel better."

The Judge said, "I know, but why did you make me say those things about three of the dearest friends I ever had?"

Remarks to Local 1272,
United Steelworkers of America
Union Hall, Pittsburgh
April 24, 1964

Fund-Raising

Looking over the crowd at a fund-raising dinner in Detroit, Lyndon Johnson spotted Henry Ford II, Chairman of the Ford Motor Company, and John F. Gordon, President of General Motors, at a nearby table. Johnson quipped, when he got up to speak:

I'm proud, happy, and stimulated that there is a Ford in my future. And with Jack Gordon here tonight, I hope there will be a Chevy, too.

1964 Campaign

At the $1,000 Democratic Gala to erase the party's million-dollar deficit, Vice President Johnson said:

This is the first act that's come to town that could really compete with the one-woman show that's packing them in down at the art gallery.*

Washington, D. C.
January 18, 1963

Mr. President, Senator Williams, Senator Bayh, Mrs. Peterson, my good friends of this great convention:

I am unaccustomed to such large crowds and such unrestrained enthusiasm. I have been addressing some of these $100 victory Democratic dinners down in Washington, and after a fellow pays that much for a ticket he doesn't have quite as much enthusiasm as you have here today.

Remarks to the 19th Constitutional Convention
of the United Auto Workers of America,
Convention Hall, Atlantic City, New Jersey
March 23, 1964

The Great Society

Let's let them come in here and talk about socialism. When I went to Washington under President Roosevelt in 1933, when he was talking about keeping the banks

* Da Vinci's "Mona Lisa."

from being closed, and he was trying to reopen them again, when he had the soup lines, when he had the CCC, when he was trying to do things where people didn't starve to death, they just talked about socialism, socialism, and finally one old boy said, "You can't eat socialism."

Los Angeles
October 28, 1964

Hard Work

Originally we scheduled this evening as an end-of-Congress get-together. In view of the developments at your end of Pennsylvania Avenue, we have redesignated tonight as a night of mid-session hospitality.

Perhaps we will be able this year to combine our farewell-to-Congress party with the annual Christmas Tree lighting ceremony.

Remarks at salute to Congress
South Lawn, The White House
August 19, 1964

The White House gardeners were anxious for me to make this trip to the Appalachian states. They said they wanted me out of town long enough so that they could cut the grass in the flower garden.

Remarks honoring J. Edgar Hoover
on his 40th anniversary
as director of the F.B.I.
Rose Garden, The White House
May 8, 1964

Health

When he went to examine the new gym at the Rayburn House Office Building, some of the Congressmen asked if he would like to "try out" some of the new equipment. The President declined:

I get a *real* workout every day in my present job.

Washington Evening Star,
March 12, 1965

Once when he was called, "the luckiest man alive," President Johnson replied:

Yes, and I find that the harder I work, the luckier I get.

Ben H. Bagdikian
Saturday Evening Post

Even about his heart attack, Mr. Johnson had a sense of humor. When he was being carted away in an ambulance in 1955, the doctor told Johnson he could not have any more cigarettes. The Senate Majority Leader said, "Take away my seniority, but don't take my cigarettes." (However, he hasn't smoked since.)

When he was at his sickest at Bethesda Naval Hospital, the tailor phoned to asked if some suits he'd ordered should be finished. "Tell him to go ahead with the dark blue one," said the Majority Leader with a weak grin. "Wherever I am, I can always use that."

July, 1955

I almost put off my physical examination the other day because I watched these commentators and I read these various analytical pieces by some of the ablest men in the country whom I had known well for many years. I was afraid my blood pressure would be too high to have an examination at that time.

Democratic Convention
Atlantic City
August 28, 1964

All things are possible when God lets loose a thinker and a doer in this world. In my opinion, Admiral Rickover is that kind of a man. His heart attack in 1961 only briefly slowed him down.

As a matter of fact, it may well be said, after seeing

what Admiral Rickover has done recently, that heart attacks are really good for you these days.

Remarks upon conferring American Heart Association's
Heart of the Year Award
Cabinet Room, The White House
January 30, 1964

H. H. H.

Vice President Humphrey backed up too close to an airplane gas heater in Georgia, and set his coattails afire, giving LBJ the perfect opening. As Humphrey stood by, blushing, the President said:

I see where he [Humphrey] has been down in Georgia this weekend getting *heated up* for the days ahead.

Presidential Conference on Council on Aging
The White House
February 16, 1965

Inaugural 1965

The culmination of his career came when LBJ was sworn in to be President as a result of the mandate of the people—a landslide victory.

He was jubilant at the Inaugural Balls, and paused at

the Sheraton-Park Hotel to get off a few good ones. "Never before have so many paid so much to dance so little," said he, surveying the congestion on the dance floor.

He added, "One thing you can say about the great society—it sure is crowded."

A little later, introducing members of the Cabinet, he said, "The Secretary of the Treasury is in charge of taking half your money and the Attorney General sues you for the other half."

Inaugural Ball
Sheraton-Park Hotel
January 20, 1965

At the Statler-Hilton Hotel, the President looked at Hubert Humphrey, who had been, by then, Vice President for less than twelve hours, and said, "There he is—the greatest Vice President I have ever known."

Statler-Hilton Hotel
January 20, 1965

Introductions

This is one of the best introductions I ever received—probably *the* best introduction I ever had, except upon one other occasion, when I was speaking

down in the hills of Tennessee and the Governor was supposed to introduce me. He did not get there, and I had to introduce myself.

After being introduced
by Dr. Milton Eisenhower
at Johns Hopkins University, Baltimore
October 1, 1964

Sometimes it falls to the President to act as toastmaster:

Ladies, I think I should, before I say the few words that I have selected to say this morning, tell you that I was just introduced in the fewest words, the shortest amount of time, by one of the greatest and ablest Secretaries of Labor that this country ever produced.

Now I want to present to you my own Secretary of War—Lady Bird.

Remarks to the League of Women Voters
Pittsburgh Hilton Hotel, Pittsburgh
April 24, 1964

When Lyndon Johnson was asked once to introduce Senator Carl Hayden at a dinner in his home state of Arizona, which Hayden had represented since it be-

came a state in 1912, LBJ made the perfect introduc-
tion:

I don't believe that Adam had to be formally introduced to Eve.

Favorite LBJ anecdote of Drew Pearson

The Irish and the English

The President has much to say about the Irish:

I know that I have become an Irishman by osmosis.

Exchange of toasts
with His Excellency, Eamon De Valera,
President of Ireland
May 27, 1964

I woke up this morning and suddenly realized that
the Irish have taken over the Government. The speaker
of the House of Representatives is a distinguished Irishman from Boston named John McCormack. The very
effective Majority Leader of the United States is an
Irishman from Montana, Mike Mansfield. And where-
ever I turn all day long, there are Kenny O'Donnell and
Larry O'Brien—and Dave Powers and Dick McGuire,
and John Bailey and George Reedy and Ralph Dungan,

the White House Chapter of the Friendly Sons of St. Patrick.

Remarks to Friendly Sons of St. Patrick
Waldorf-Astoria Hotel, New York City
March 17, 1964

And the English:

During World War II, the British Minister in Algeria was called upon to mediate a dispute between British and American officers.

The American officers wanted drinks served before their meals. The British wanted their drinks served after their meals. He came up with this answer: "In deference to the British," he said, "we will all drink after meals, and in deference to the Americans, we will all drink before the meal."

This kind of British genius has solved a great many problems.

Statement by the President
during exchange of toasts
with Prime Minister Harold Wilson
State Dining Room, The White House
December 7, 1964

And the Scotch:

You might well ask how it was that the two of us hit it off so well together, one a Scots Highlander and the other a Texas rancher, but you must remember that Sir Alec and I are really countrymen—although he prefers Black Angus and I prefer Herefords, and although his countryside gets too much rain, while mine gets too little.

Remarks at White House state dinner
for The Right Honorable Sir Alec Douglas-Home,
Prime Minister of the United Kingdom
February 13, 1964

The Kennedys

Speaking of Jacqueline Kennedy, Vice President Johnson said:

She is a one woman REA* who has electrified America.

Dedication of Treaty Room
The White House
June 29, 1962

When First Lady Jacqueline Kennedy was redecorating the White House, she prevailed on Vice President Johnson to return the historic chandelier which had been removed from the White House during the Theodore Roosevelt Administration and taken to the Senate. At the dedication of the Treaty Room, where Mrs. Ken-

* Rural Electrification Administration.

nedy had hung the chandelier, Johnson explained the background of the historic move:

The story goes that Teddy Roosevelt, before they had air conditioning, was troubled by the wind blowing the chandelier pieces together and the noise of the prisms chiming whenever anyone opened a door or a window. He ordered his men to take it down to the butler. The butler said, "Well, what will I do with it?"

"Send it to the Vice President," Teddy Roosevelt growled. "He never has anything to do, and the tinkling will keep him awake."

The Vice President then grinned at the First Lady, and added:

I guess now there will be some who say that we want it back in the White House to keep the President awake.

Treaty Room
The White House
June 29, 1962

President Johnson has always admired all the Kennedy wives, and still does. During the 1964 campaign in Massachusetts he said:

I think that Ted Kennedy ought to be enshrined among the successful men of our time if for one reason alone: He had the good fortune to marry Joan.

October 27, 1964

Kids

I know some of you would agree with a little boy—
the son of a big businessman—who said that capital
punishment is "when the Government sets up business

in competition with you, and then takes all your profit with taxes in order to make up its loss."

Remarks at meeting with business leaders
The White House
1964

A little boy down in our county who was having quite a problem with his family's eating wrote the Lord one day and said, "Dear Lord: I wish you would send mother a hundred dollars to help us get along."

The letter wound up in Washington on the Postmaster General's desk.

The Postmaster General still had a little money left in his billfold and pulled out a $20 bill and sent it back to the little boy.

A few days later he got another letter from the little fellow, and it said:

"Dear Lord: I want to say much obliged for that twenty bucks you sent us. The next time, though, please don't send it through Washington because they took a deduct of 80 percent."

So we won't have any deducts on our meeting here today.

Remarks before United Workers
March 23, 1964

Lady Bird

I had some very special advice, Mr. Prime Minister, just a few minutes before you arrived. My wife whis-

pered in my ear as we were coming out to greet you this morning.

She said, "Dear, this is *Judgment* Day and be sure you use plenty of it."

During visit of Prime Minister Harold Wilson
December, 1964

The first thing I want to do is to present to you a lady who lost her salary the day that I took the oath of office as President, but one who is not unemployed—Lady Bird.

Remarks to Local 1272,
United Steelworkers of America,
Union Hall, Pittsburgh
April 24, 1964

For Lady Bird's 51st birthday, the President gave her a photograph of himself with an inscription that paraphrased one he had given her twenty-nine years before, during their courtship:

"For Bird, still a girl of principles, ideals and refinement—from her admirer, Lyndon."

December 22, 1963

I am glad that Mrs. Johnson asked me to speak, I thought of the story of the man and his wife who were having an argument. The man's neighbor said to him, "I understand that you and Mary had some words."

He said, "Yes, I had some, but I didn't get to use mine."

I appreciate Lady Bird giving me a chance to use some of my words this afternoon.

Remarks to foreign students
The White House
May 5, 1964

Lawyers

Mr. Attorney General and Mrs. Kennedy, ladies and gentlemen: With your wives and children here this morning this almost has the appearance of another White House press conference.

As for those of you who left your families at home, maybe you can get a good lawyer to defend you when you return.

Someone once said that lawyers are like bread—they are best when they are young and fresh.

Remarks at meeting with U. S. Attorneys,
East Room, The White House
July 8, 1964

Letters from LBJ

LBJ loves to write letters when he is amused When Secretary of the Treasury Douglas Dillon retired from government after a lengthy career that included a stint as Ambassador to France, he announced that he and his wife were going on a long, long vacation abroad. Presi-

dent Johnson gave a farewell dinner and read a copy
of a letter he had "sent" to Dillon's wife:

Dear Phyllis:

I have today received and read with care your con-
cise and succinct letter and I appreciate all eighteen
pages of it.

I hope you will permit me to reply to several of the
allegations you have made in your letter.

First, it is not true that I plan to announce at the
White House dinner on Thursday your husband's ac-
ceptance of another job. I promised him firmly—that I
would not announce it until you both are in the air.

Second, it was your husband, not me, who thought
up the idea that Americans should travel at home
rather than abroad—and it was Senator Fulbright, not
me, who said Americans should be careful about what
happens to them in Paris.

Third, when I said in my letter to your husband that
Americans are in his debt, I was not implying that the
books don't balance.

Fourth, neither I nor anyone else objects to Doug
leaving Washington—but a President has many bur-
dens, Phyllis, and I am going to have much explaining
to do if I let *you* go, at the *same* time . . .

Favorite LBJ letter of Betty Beale,
Washington Star

The new president of the National Press Club, Bill
Blair of the New York Times, *received one of LBJ's*

humorous letters when he, like Mr. Johnson, took office in January, 1965:

THE WHITE HOUSE
WASHINGTON, D.C.

January 25, 1965

Dear Bill:

It has come to my attention through a leak (or a drip) from the headquarters of the White House Correspondents' Assn., that you are shortly to assume the exalted position of President of the National Press Club. As one who has had some experience in a comparable field, I feel that I should accustom you early to one of the major functions of such an office—receiving unsolicited advice.

I do not know how you feel about the question of proper attire for the Inauguration. This, I believe, could properly be left to your own discretion (providing you first consult the suit rental industry to avoid an economic crisis). But I would like to suggest that you take the oath of office in an atmosphere that befits the solemnity and decorum of the high occasion. Perhaps you could begin by turning immediately to the "State of the Press Club" message to your constituents.

It should start with an announcement of your firm intention to institute an economy program—perhaps through reducing the size of NPC beverage glasses and turning out the lights in the East Lounge at an early hour. For many years, I have speculated on the glow that emanates from the upper stories of the building as I have driven past between the Capitol and the White House. Even though I have been assured by knowledgeable members of my staff that the radiance comes from a source other than the Washington Power & Light Co., it would still be worth looking into.

Next, of course, there is the question of stimulating the economy. This was performed, in my instance, by a tax cut. I do not presume to present you with a detailed outline of parallel action on your part. But I believe that if you and your board of directors were to institute a similar move, it would be greeted with great enthusiasm.

Next, you should drive home to the members of the National Press Club the realization that the Great Society can be achieved only through united action by all segments of the economy of the Fourth Estate. This concept may encounter opposition from the conservative element of another era, but I believe that if you reason together you can achieve the necessary consensus—even with the Women's National Press Club.

Finally, a bit of personal advice. Shorten the service hours if you will, increase the price of food, shut down on all Sundays and holidays, and you still might survive. But whatever you do, don't, under any circumstances, allow dogs on the premises.

> Best regards,
> LYNDON JOHNSON

Air Conditioning, Heating & Refrigeration News
April 5, 1965

Lights

In the White House Rose Garden, the President once told a group:

Ladies and gentlemen, I appreciate your coming here today. The reason I wanted you in the Rose Garden is simply because if we had gone inside the White House Lady Bird would have insisted that I turn on all the lights.

We are going into the White House shortly, so you can pick up your candles in a box over there.

Remarks to the American Society
of Newspaper Editors,
Rose Garden, The White House,
April 17, 1964

To sit down and exchange views with you from time to time is vital to the health of our free enterprise economy. For one thing, it keeps the light bill up—and the electric companies like that!

And for another thing, it keeps me off the streets— and *Time* magazine likes that!

Remarks at the Business Leaders' Dinner
Washington, D. C.
April 28, 1964

Lady Bird was glad to hear that you were coming today. She said to me this morning, "Please, Lyndon, for these fellows, let us turn on the lights today."

You probably heard that the Republicans have urged people to send me a penny to pay the White House light bill. Well, that far-reaching campaign, I think, for the Republicans was very successful. They forwarded 150 pennies. That is about the way most Republican campaigns operate.

Among the pennies that came in yesterday I found a letter from Barry Goldwater. Barry was generous, much more generous than the average Republican. He sent more than a penny. He sent a nickel, a wooden nickel.

Remarks to Cooperative League of the U. S. A.,
Rose Garden, The White House
May 20, 1964

Miss Carper [President of the Women's National Press Club], Judge Kross, Ambassador Stevenson, Justice Black, Miss Perkins, members of th Roosevelt family, distinguished guests, my fellow Americans: I came here tonight on the positive assurance of Elsie Carper that I could count this appearance as another press conference.

Unaccustomed as I am to bright lights, it is good to be able to see all of you again.

I think I should tell you that the stories they write about the White House being in the dark are greatly exaggerated.

There is some truth in the statement that Linda and Luci do study by kerosene lamps occasionally, but it is on the ranch and not in Washington. But when the sun comes up, we always open the curtains.

Statler Hilton Hotel, Washington, D. C.
March 4, 1964

One day while electricians were working at the White House they were annoyed when the lights suddenly went off in the room in which they were working. Then the lights went back on again and then off again.

"What fool is monkeying around with the light switch?" exclaimed one of the electricians.

As he opened the door to look, he found himself eyeball to eyeball with the President of the United States. The President explained that he was trying to turn off the lights in two unoccupied rooms and the embarrassed electrician explained that the lights in all three rooms were on the same switch.

"Well," said the President, with a twinkle in his eye, "We don't want any fools around the White House, so let's have separate switches installed for each room."

Favorite LBJ Anecdote of Maurice Silverman,
Department of Justice

Luci and Lynda

My daughter Luci is very interested in science—not political science either, although she adapts herself where necessary to it.

When I told her I was going to meet you, she congratulated me. She said, "Daddy, there's nothing more 'in' than brains."

Remarks to Westinghouse Science Education
Foundation's High School Science Talent Winners
March 1, 1965

In 1959, when LBJ was majority leader, Inga, a
popular local TV personality asked him, "Since you're
the boss at your office and such a big one at that, who is
the boss in your house?" Johnson replied:

Well, Lady Bird, Lynda Bird and Luci Baines divide that authority between them.

Favorite Johnson story of Inga Rundvold,
star of "Today with Inga" (WRC-NBC)

About Luci, the President says:
I never know when she's going to do what her father does instead of what her mother would like both of us to do.

12th Annual International Azalea Festival
Norfolk, Virginia
April 24, 1965

My older daughter, who came in with us, who is really my "college authority in residence," gave me a good many instructions about what to say to you today. She said, "Now, Daddy, don't give them your usual stuff. Don't tell them how well the economy is doing, because after this trip to Washington they are all going to be broke anyway. And don't talk about the beauties of frugality, because those of us living on college allowances already know about frugality." She did say that I could leave the lights on until it gets dark tonight.

Remarks to college student leaders
The White House
October 3, 1964

Noticing Lynda's billowy muu-muu dress, which puffed her out in the middle, especially since it had pouched pockets, the President clasped his hands around her tummy and told newsmen, "She's not what she looks like."

Johnson Ranch
Johnson City, Texas
Christmas, 1963

Philosophy

Whenever any of his colleagues in the Senate would
be especially foxy or verbally dexterous to obscure

*his position on an issue, Senate Democratic Leader
Johnson would recall this story:*

A schoolteacher was applying for a position down in
the hill country of Texas. He came before the school
board and a member of the school board said, "There is
some difference of opinion in our community about
geography. We want to know where you stand—do you
think that the world is round, or that it is flat?"

The applicant thought a moment and then replied,
"I can teach it either way."

*Theodore Irwin, Family Weekly,
October 18, 1964*

"My intention," President Johnson once said, "is to
get my advice from the old men and my actions from
the young."

*The White House
1963*

Politics

There is no doubt in my mind that nothing could
have been started until the Irish invented politics.

This is supposed to be a non-partisan gathering, so I
won't mention the fact that the Democratic Party is
peaceful these days. As a matter of fact, it is so peace-

ful, the Irish may move to the Republican Party where the feuding is really going on.

Remarks to Friendly Sons of St. Patrick,
Waldorf-Astoria Hotel, New York City,
March 17, 1964

I think that it is very important that we have a two-party country. I am a fellow who likes small parties, and the Republican Party is about the size I like.

Alvin Shuster, New York Times Magazine,
September 13, 1964

Preacher Stories

Preacher stories and stories with a touch of religion are LBJ's favorite humor. This is the President's favorite preacher story, and he tells it often to make a point:

I don't want you to answer me like the man who always slept through the preacher's sermon down in my hill country. Every Sunday he would come and get on the front row and snore all during the sermon.

Finally the preacher got a little irritated, and one Sunday he said, "All the people—" the fellow was snoring in the front row. He said in a low voice, "All you people who want to go to Heaven, please rise."

Everyone stood up except the man who was asleep. When they sat down, the preacher said in a very loud voice that was calculated to arouse him, "All of you men that want to go to hell, please stand up."

The man jumped up. He looked around in back of him.

He looked at the preacher, somewhat frustrated, and he said, "Preacher, I don't know what it is we are voting on, but you and me seem to be the only two for it."

Montana's Centennial
Rose Garden, The White House
April 17, 1964

I heard the story last night of the woman who telephoned her bank. She wanted to arrange for the disposal of a $1,000 bond. The clerk asked her, "Madam, is the bond for redemption or conversion?" There was a very long pause, and then the woman said, "Well, am I talking to the First National Bank or the First Baptist Church?"

President's Committee on Equal Employment Opportunity
Indian Treaty Room, Executive Office Building
May 12, 1964

When signing an education bill on a Sunday:

My Attorney General advises me that it is legal, and my minister advises me that it is moral, to sign today.

April, 1965

The President likes to say:

If God is willing and the Congress approves . . .

I rise to speak, remembering the most popular preacher who ever came to our Texas hill country. His popularity was due, he said, to the fact that he offered a silent prayer for himself each Sunday morning before his sermon.

It went like this:

> "Lord, fill my mouth
> With worthwhile stuff,
> And nudge me when
> I've said enough."

Presidential Prayer Breakfast
Washington, D. C.
March, 1961

Johnson takes delight in having not one, but two former preachers on his staff—Bill Moyers and Brooks Hays:

I wish you could have seen Billy Graham and Bill Moyers in that [White House] pool together the other day. Everyone else was already a Christian, so they just took turns baptizing each other.

I want you to know that Hays and Moyers are faithful to the cause, though. I go around turning out the lights, and they keep reminding me that the Scripture says to "let your light so shine." I just replied that the Scripture also says that "The children of this world are in their generation wiser than the children of light."

Remarks to a Group from the Christian
Leadership Seminar of Southern Baptists
Rose Garden, The White House
March 25, 1964

Many wonder where Johnson got his favorite expres-
sion, "Come, let us reason together." As he tells it, it
happened like this, and incidentally, it is Lady Bird's
favorite LBJ story:

One time when I got in a fight with a head of a power company that wouldn't let me build a little REA line in my country district in Texas, I said, "As far as I am concerned, you can take a running jump and go straight to you know where!"

Everybody in my REA and public power group applauded me, and thought I was brave and great. One old man, though, the general counsel for the water district, who had been a lawyer a long time, and mighty wise, and had been in a lot of fights, didn't applaud. He looked serious. He was an ex-Senator.

I said, "Senator, what did you think of my speech?"

He said, "Come to my office and I will tell you."

I went by his office and he said, "Young man, you are just starting in public life. I hope you are in it a long time. I hope you go a long way. But the first thing you have to learn is this: *Telling a man to go to hell and then making him go are two different propositions."*

He said, "First of all, it is hot down there, and the average fellow doesn't want to go, and when you tell him he *has* to go, he just bristles up, and he is a lot less likely to go than if you hadn't told him anything.

"What you better do is get out the Good Book that your Mama used to read to you and go back to the prophet Isaiah and read what he said. He said, 'Come now, let us reason together.' "

South Gate, California
October 11, 1964

Explaining that he didn't have a prepared speech with him that day, LBJ said:

We had a preacher back home who dropped his notes just as he was leaving for his church one time, and his dog jumped at them and tore them up.

When the preacher went to the pulpit, he apologized to his congregation and said, "I am very sorry, today I have no sermon. I will just have to speak as the Lord directs. But I will try to do better next Sunday."

I don't have a speech today. I just intend to do as George Reedy directed at the press conference this morning—to speak as the Lord directs.

American Society of Newspaper Editors
April 17, 1964

The Presidency

At his first press conference, this exchange took place:

Question: Mr. President, can you tell us at the end of your first two weeks in office what you regard as the biggest single problem facing you as President?
The President: Being President.

December 7, 1963

But I want you to know this: that no one person, not even with Lady Bird and Lynda Bird and Luci Baines to help him, can lead this nation by himself.

South Gate, California
October 11, 1964

As my counselor Ted Sorensen wrote in his new book: "In the White House, the future rapidly becomes the past, and delay is in itself a decision."

Remarks before the Business Advisory Council
December 4, 1963

It was said of Abraham Lincoln that one time he sat distressed before his Cabinet, and he decided he would take a vote. He called the roll of the Cabinet, and each man answered in a loud and clear voice, "Nay."
Finally, when all the members of the Cabinet had

had their names called and all had voted "Nay", the President called his own name and he voted "aye." Then he said, "The ayes have it."

Well, I thought of that story when I was making up the budget for this canal.

Remarks at ground-breaking ceremonies
of the Cross-Florida Barge Canal,
Palatka, Florida
February 27, 1964

The Press

Mr. Chancellor, in a few moments now I am going to turn you over to the American press, and then I think you will know how the deer feel.

At a barbecue in honor
of Chancellor Ludwig Erhard of West Germany
Stonewall, Texas
December 29, 1963

I wanted to be a teacher, and was until the pay scale pushed me into the line of work that I am now in. I never went as far as Teddy Roosevelt, who said of the Vice Presidency that he would greatly rather be anything else, even a professor of history.

Also, I can assure you that at times, especially after I read the newspapers, I have strong urges to be a writer.

In fact, if I may turn the tables, I sometimes think some of my friends in the press need some new writers.

Fish Room, The White House
April 30, 1964

We have got a great system in this country. We can worship God according to the dictates of our conscience. We have free speech. We have free press—and it never gets quite as free as it does during Convention time.

National Democratic Committee
Atlantic City
August 28, 1964

Shortly after the report had been published that he had been driving like a racing driver and throwing beer cans out of the car, he was the guest of the very people who had put the shaft to him. The President took the rousing ovation at the reception very good-humoredly:

I want to thank you fellows, but I just don't understand how a group of men who are being so nice in the evening can be so mean during working hours.

Favorite LBJ story of Adm. John Harllee,
Chairman, Federal Maritime Commission
Reception for Government Executives,
National Press Club,
April 7, 1964

I was at the Gridiron Club and they were roasting all of us. I said I don't know whether a fellow is safer being a guest of the newspaper people or whether he is worse off having them as his guests.

Washington, D.C.
April, 1964

At a White House press conference, this exchange took place:

Question: Mr. President, the Republicans have a new slogan referring to you as "LBJ—Light Bulb Johnson." Would you call that a knock or a boost?
The President: I would call that plagiarizing the *Washington Post.*

The White House
April 12, 1964

The reporters who cover the President's lengthy walks around the White House grounds have nicknamed it "the death march." As for the President, he says:

You may not be able to tell it by just looking at them, but I want to give my personal testimony, in behalf of the newspapermen and newspaperwomen, that they are doing very well in our own White House physical fitness training program on our daily walks.

The President pins a so-called "Purple Heart" (actually an LBJ button) on reporter Peter Lisagor of the *Chicago Daily News* for an injury sustained during one of the famous walks around the White House grounds. Lisagor walked into a lamp post on the first lap.

We have had very few casualties—we lost one or two high heels, had one or two drop-outs—but generally speaking, the marks are high. Give me a little more time and both the press and, I hope, the President will be in better shape.

Remarks at ceremony honoring
physical fitness winners
Rose Garden, The White House
May 3, 1965

I am very happy that you requested through the Press Office this opportunity for us to meet together, because after looking at some of the cartoons you've drawn, I thought I'd invite you over to see me in person. After all, I had nothing to lose.

Association of American Editorial Cartoonists
May 13, 1965

Progress

It was called to my attention recently that in 1861 a speed record was set in delivering the Inaugural Address of President Lincoln to the West Coast. Using Pony Express, copies of Lincoln's address were delivered from Washington to California in seven days and seventeen hours, by seventy-five ponies, at a cost of five dollars per one-half ounce.

Today, for only five cents we can send three ounces of Presidential addresses across the country—at about the same rate of speed.

Remarks at swearing-in ceremony
for John A. Gronouski
Cabinet Room, The White House
February 19, 1965

I understand that at the close of this fair a time capsule will be placed in the ground. Every possible precaution has been taken to make sure that it will be

opened several thousand years from now. Special met-
als have been used. Records of its location will be
stored around the world. They have only neglected one
vital precaution. They do not have an advance com-
mitment from Robert Moses that when the time finally
comes, he will let them dig it up.

Remarks at opening of World's Fair
New York City
April 22, 1964

Laughing at himself and his willingness to take
credit, Johnson said this when Postmaster General
John Gronouski promised one-day mail service any-
where in the United States:

I am for it.

I would only point out that until that promise is ful-
filled, I want the press to duly record that it is John
Gronouski's promise, not mine.

But if it does come to pass, it will be the record of the
Johnson Administration.

Washington, D.C.
February, 1965

Back in World War I, a representative of the American Chemical Society called on the Secretary of War
and offered the services of the nation's chemists. The
Secretary thanked him and asked him to return the next
day. When he did, the Secretary of War expressed ap-

preciation for the offer but said it was unnecessary. He had looked into the matter and he had found that the War Department already had a scientist.

Remarks to winners of the Science Talent Search, Cabinet Room, The White House
March 1, 1965

Quips

Mr. Nixon would look after TVA like a fox would look after chickens.

Jackson, Tennessee
September 30, 1960

The Democrats have elephant memories.

Remarks to Labor Press Seminar Group
East Room, The White House
April 27, 1964

We don't all see everything alike. If we did, we would all want the same wife.

Los Angeles
October, 1964

- My definition for *off the record* is that you don't even tell it at the Press Club bar.

Favorite LBJ quip of Frances Spatz Leighton

The LBJ Ranch

The President was roasted in the press for his fast driving around the Texas countryside, can of beer in hand. But he had the last laugh:

There is something good that comes out of everything. When lightning struck Lady Bird's plane out in Cleveland the other day, it scared us for a moment, but a lot of good came out of it. She is willing to start riding with me again now.

But anyway, we put in a new rule at the LBJ Ranch —if I ever get to go down there—I have just been down there twice in five months. A crisis seems to develop every week, nearly, and they [the press] would really ruin me if I happened to be there when a crisis developed, but I will tell you one thing for sure: If any of you show up at the LBJ Ranch, we have some new rules. Everybody is going to walk from now on, and I am going to do what Lady Bird tells me, and we are going to make everybody drink nothing but pure rain water or Pepsi-Cola.

Constitution Hall
Washington, D.C.
April, 1964

The Staff

This is, after all, your house—even if Brooks Hays and Bill Moyers think it belongs to them.

If you wonder why Brooks and Bill are both around, I just want to assure you that I am trying to be scriptural. A proverb of the Old Testament says, "In a multitude of counselors there is safety."

Brooks keeps telling me that it really meant, "In a multitude of Baptist counselors." Everyone, I think, knows that two Baptists make a multitude.

If you doubt their influence, I urge you to read last week's *Saturday Evening Post*. There is an article in there, and they are usually accurate, which says that all three of the new staff members that Johnson brought to the White House are Protestants.

It so happens that two of the three are Catholics. The only conclusion I could reach after reading that article is Bill Moyers converted those two other fellows and baptized them in a mighty big hurry. Of course, that is why I keep the swimming pool full all the time.

Remarks to a group from the Christian
Leadership Seminar of Southern Baptists
Rose Garden, The White House
March 25, 1964

Twenty-seven years ago this month I came here as a newly-elected Congressman aboard the train with Franklin Roosevelt. . . .

Washington has changed very little since then. Not long ago I called in one of the very bright and very busy young men I have working with me, and I said to him, rather brusquely, because I was in a hurry, "The people want to know what we are going to do about the farm bill. Let's get our recommendations up right away."

He came right back and said, "Mr. President, I don't think we have to consider that. I don't have a file on it. I will look it up, but I think you ought to go tell them if we owe it, we will pay it."

Remarks to U. S. Chamber of Commerce
Constitution Hall, Washington, D.C.
April 27, 1964

Introducing Dr. Walter W. Heller, his chief economic adviser, who was leaving for financial reasons, the President cracked:

I've got an economic adviser who needs an economic adviser. He's broke.

The White House
April, 1964

There is a story about Johnson and his staff which shows the frantic work pace around the White House. One evening the President had need for someone from his staff to help him on some matters.

He called for one member of his staff and was informed that he was celebrating his wedding anniversary with his wife that evening.

He called for a second member and was told that that staff member was celebrating his wife's birthday that evening.

He called for a third member of the staff and was told that he was attending a school play in which his young daughter was playing. Exclaimed the President "What I need around here are some bachelors."

Favorite LBJ story of Maurice Silverman,
Department of Justice

The Telephone

Johnson's telephone has made a happier woman of a Queens, Long Island, housewife. Her telephone number is the same as that of the White House, except for the area code number—it's 212 in New York and 202 in Washington—and she keeps getting the President's phone calls—456-1414.

She used to be a little lonely because she didn't have many relatives, but the White House calls have changed all that, and to quote Rose Brown, "When people call my number we get into conversation. It's good therapy. I'd be lost now without it. It has become part of me. It really has. I love people."

And what kind of calls does she get? Well, one little boy told her, "We're very poor and I would like the President to send $4." And another child was willing to settle for just a picture of the President.

It was bound to happen that the President, himself,

would hear of the goings-on, and he did. He sent a note to Mrs. Brown which showed his wry humor:

". . . if you will do the best that you can in handling White House calls, I assure you we will do the best that we can in handling the calls for the Brown family."

Washington Star
May 2, 1965

Texas and Texans

My Friends and Fellow Democrats:

I come tonight as a Senator from the largest state in the Union—south of the North Pole.

Contrary to what you may have heard, Texans welcome Alaska as an outlying state. We are glad to find a state that can outlie us.

I could not feel more at home than I do here.

Welch, West Virginia
October 18, 1958

In the early part of the nineteenth century my grandmother's people all lived in Kentucky. We just came over here from Martin County, and that was a family name.

My mother told me that my early ancestors reached Kentucky and were told there were two ways to go up: They could either go up in the world or they could go to Texas.

Paintsville, Kentucky
April 24, 1964

The White House

About the White House, LBJ has said, with humor tinged with pain, that, in effect, a public house is not a home, even if it's a White *House:*

It's *not* a home. It's a place where you go when you finish work. Airplanes flying in and out of National Airport wake you up at five A.M. And if that doesn't happen, tourists are going right under your bed by eight in the morning.

And if you try to take a nap in the afternoon, Lady Bird and Laurence Rockefeller and eighty women are in the next room talking about how the daffodils are doing on Pennsylvania Avenue.

The White House
May 4, 1965

Women

When Margaret Price called me and asked me to come over to speak to the Democratic women, I told

her that would be a switch, because I have been listening to them for the past thirty years.

Remarks to the 1964 Campaign
Conference for Democratic Women
Sheraton-Park Hotel, Washington, D.C.
April 30, 1964

Someone once said that the Lord made the universe and rested. The Lord made man and rested. The Lord made woman—and since then neither the Lord nor man has rested. That is what the Republican candidates have found out in New Hampshire ever since Margaret Chase Smith came on the scene.

Remarks at Democratic Party Dinner
Fontainebleau Hotel, Miami Beach
February 27, 1964

I am sure that all of you already understand my very strong conviction, to which Lady Bird has referred, that we must make more use of the talents of women in government if we expect to have better government.

One lady, Senator Margaret Smith, did misunderstand my feelings about this. I was talking about the echelon *below* the Presidency. I *never thought* that Margaret would think that I was really talking about *my* job—at least not for the time being.

Remarks before League of Women Voters
Pittsburgh Hilton Hotel, Pittsburgh
April 24, 1964

Our country has come a long way since the first woman government employee was appointed Postmaster at Baltimore in 1773. She was Mary Goddard.

Miss Goddard faced rather formidable opposition. At that time, no less a person than Thomas Jefferson was saying, and I quote:

"The appointment of a woman to office is an innovation for which the public is not prepared."

Remarks at Federal Women's Award Ceremony
Cabinet Room, The White House
March 2, 1965

Many people had doubts and fears when I began the program of recruiting women. I want to report to you tonight that those fears were entirely unfounded and unjustified. We have not had to install more than one powder room in each Federal building. We have had to hire only a very few babysitters. And our Bureau of Husband Complaints needs only three people to handle the calls.

Bringing women into the Government has even increased new job opportunities for men. There is more of a demand these days for male secretaries then ever before.

Remarks to the 1964 Campaign
Conference for Democratic Women
Sheraton-Park Hotel, Washington, D.C.
April 30, 1964

A writer once observed, a bit critically, that American women seek a perfection in their husbands that English women find only in their butlers. But that only proves to me that American women have a taste for style and a yearning for excellence.

Eleanor Roosevelt Candlestick
Award Dinner
March 4, 1964

I don't want the male members of our party to be worried. They will always have a place in the Federal Government as long as there is no woman to fill the job.

Remarks to the 1964 Campaign
Conference for Democratic Women
Sheraton-Park Hotel, Washington, D.C.
April 30, 1964

Zeal and Zealmanship

When Johnson was a young congressman in the U. S. House of Representatives, he tried to get as many bills passed to help his district as possible, and eventually he had a bill in for a dam. As he tells the story:

When the debate started before the House, I went to the old chairman of the Public Works Committee and said, "Do I make my speech now?"

The old chairman said, "Not yet."

I went to him a few minutes later and got the same answer. This happened five or six times.

Finally I went over to the old man and stressed my desire to make a speech. The old fellow held up his finger like that, and just at that point the clerk read off this particular dam and the House approved it.

Again I said, "But when do I make my speech?"

The old chairman said, "Young man, when you go down to dedicate the dam."

Favorite LBJ story of Congressman Claude Pepper of Florida

In 1861 a certain Texan left to join the rebels, telling his neighbors he'd return soon. The fight would be easy, he said, "because we can lick those damyankees with broomsticks."

Two years later, he returned bedraggled, and neighbors wanted to know what happened.

"The trouble was," he said, "the damyankees wouldn't fight with broomsticks!"

Favorite LBJ story of Mike Trupp, Federal Maritime Commission

Registering disappointment at the unveiling of a portrait of Senator Abraham Ribicoff, Johnson ruefully said, "I was told that they were going to hang *a United States Senator."*

When the laughter had subsided, the President continued:

One day not so long ago, I was asked by one of my assistants if I would like to attend a hanging.

I was understandably hesitant. But I did inquire who was to be the honoree.

I was told that they were going to hang a United States Senator, my old, good and warm friend of many years, Abe Ribicoff.

I said—with caution befitting a former Senator—"You better double-check that. It is just possible they got the wrong man."

Remarks at Ribicoff portrait unveiling,
Department of Health, Education and Welfare
March 3, 1965